Volume 1

The Box Breakers

STUDENT ANTHOLOGY

WITH DR. ANNISE MABRY

Chief Patricia Barber
Rachel Wall
Brandilyn Cromer
Mazie Harris
Chief Rachael Hart
Jerry Haugabook
Stephanie Johnson
Emmett Alicyn Mabry
Niles Mabry
Toronica Price
Kateisha Smith
Crystal Spence
Jessica Stephens

Box Breakers

by Dr. Annise Mabry & her Associates

© 2021 Dr. Annise Mabry Foundation & the Tiers Free Academy

www.tiersfreeacademy.org

All rights reserved. No portion of this book may be reproduced in any form without express permission from Dr. Annise Mabry Foundation.

Dedicated to the memory of Helen Harvey, Becky Wood, Jesse Barber, and Noah Anderson.

Cover Design: Aimee Andrichak Editor: Rhodora O

Ebook ISBN: 978-1-7324966-2-0 Print book ISBN: 978-1-7324966-3-7

TABLE OF CONTENTS

Preface	4
The Tiers Free Journey	6
Origins - Dr. Annise Mabry	8
Emmett - Emmett Alicyn Mabry	12
Niles - Niles Mabry	19
Beginnings - Dr. Annise Mabry	21
The Navigators - Dr. Annise Mabry	24
The Tiers Free Stories	28
Parent Story - Crystal Spence	29
Graduate Story I - Jessica Stephens	32
Thrive with Pride Story I - Brandilyn Cromer	37
Police Story I - Chief Rachael Hart	40
Graduate Story II - Rachel Wall	44
Graduate Story III - Kateisha Smith	46
Police Story II - Chief Patricia Barber	48
Graduate Story IV - Mazie Harris	52
Thrive with Pride Story II - Jerry Haugabook	55
Graduate Story V - Toronica Price	58
Graduate Story VI - Stephanie Johnson	60
Epilogue - Dr. Annise Mabry	62
SPECIAL - The Tiers Free Difference	65

Preface

They arrive in my office battered, broken, and defeated. They see me as another person in the educational system who is just going to beat them down again.

I hear it in their voices when I say, "tell me what you plan to do once you get your diploma?" They are so broken sometimes that they've stopped dreaming.

I didn't start this homeschool journey because I wanted to. I did it because this was the only tool that I had to save my own children. I used to always say, "I'm not anti-public education;" but you know what—I am. I am against everything that public education allows to happen in those classrooms. I am against those academic leaders who didn't earn their positions but were simply 'friendshipped' into those positions. Not because they were the best candidates but because they were the best networked. I used to say that I forgave the failures of leadership for how they allowed my daughter to be broken. That's a lie. I didn't forgive them and I never will.

Every time my daughter had a panic attack in a classroom, I hated those leaders even more.

There are 866,000 adults in Georgia without a high school diploma. Many of them are sex trafficking survivors, homeless LGBTQ youth, former foster care youth, and youth with untreated and undiagnosed mental illnesses. Regardless of who they are, one thing they have in common is that they are trapped inside a box—of trying to find employment without a high school diploma.

My role in their story is small—I simply built a program that provided them with a pathway to become a high school graduate. They made the choice to break the box.

They are the box breakers and this anthology is their story. Some of their stories will make you laugh and some will make you cry. Some will make you question why no one intervened to help.

What I hope to achieve with this book is that not only you take away insights and inspirations for your own life, family or community from all these stories… but you are also inspire to give back … to yourself, to your people, and to us.

Dr. Annise Mabry
Founder of
Tiers Free Academy and
The Dr. Annise Mabry Foundation

THE TIERS
FREE JOURNEY

Origins

Dr. Annise Mabry

I grew up in rural West Georgia - just 30 miles away from Clem, GA, where my mom grew up. My granddaddy was a bi-racial sharecropper in the 1940s. Rural West Georgia in the 1940s was fertile ground for not only farmers, but also for domestic terrorist groups such as the Klu Klux Klan (KKK).

But fear wasn't something that my granddaddy had because education was, and is, our family business. My granddaddy on my mother's side used to pass for white so that he could teach the black sharecroppers how to read, write and count their crops. He had gotten tired of watching the sharecroppers being cheated out of what was rightfully theirs. He felt so strongly about this that he literally risked his life to change the situation. His efforts didn't go unnoticed. When the Klu Klux Klan found out what my grandfather was doing, they organized a mob to kill him and to teach his family a lesson.

In the middle of the night, my grandfather and grandmother filled a wagon with hay and loaded their children onto this wagon. The children were told to lay flat, be still and be quiet as my grandparents carefully stacked furniture on top of them.

They never got a chance to say goodbye to their friends or neighbors, because the simple act of saying goodbye could put their neighbors in jeopardy if the KKK came looking for my grandparents.
Once the wagon was loaded, my grandfather then drove the wagon out of town. It has only been in the last five years that my mom shared this story with me.

My father's family, on the other hand, was almost the exact opposite. My dad grew up on his family's farm—which sounds normal but in the 1930s for a black person to own one acre of land was amazing. My dad's family owned almost 100 acres of land. My granddaddy was a farmer and a school bus driver.

My parents and siblings (who are 15 and 17 years older than me) attended segregated schools. In 1978, my kindergarten class was the first integrated Kindergarten class in Coweta County.

Coweta County was one of those sleepy, rural Southern towns that had the wisdom to accept federal funding for infrastructure when many rural towns opposed the funding and that made a tremendous impact on how the county supported education. In my family, children were taught that you have one job and that is to go to school. It was never a question of if you were going to graduate from high school but the expectation was not only would you graduate but that you would also continue on into college.

My brother graduated from the University of Georgia with a BS in Chemistry and enlisted in the Army. My sister attended South GA College but left college to pursue a career in law enforcement.

My brother and sister were the popular kids in high school—she was a cheerleader and he was a football player.

Growing up, my mom tried to put me into all of the activities that my sister enjoyed but that wasn't me. My sister loved dolls and I loved dirt. She loved Barbies and I loved bikes. She loved shopping for clothes and I could never seem to go one day without tearing my clothes up from jumping over a barbwire fence to ride a 4- wheeler in the creek bed. My mom and sister were close because they shared similar interests; but, my closest relationship was with my dad.

My dad was the go-to body and fender repair man for our county. Every time my dad turned on a power tool to repair a car, I was right there. Actually, anything my dad did, I was right there.

My favorite day of the week growing up was Sunday. My dad had a Honda motorcycle and every Sunday, he would take Sunday rides and as soon as I was old enough to put my own helmet on, he took me with him.

My dad never set the expectation that I shouldn't do things because I was a girl—in fact, he empowered me to do unconventional things because I was a girl and he didn't feel that there should be jobs based on gender. I used to joke that I could tape a car for painting better than I could paint makeup on my face (and that's still true—so when you see me out with flawless makeup just know that I didn't do it myself).

Another unique fact about my childhood was I only spent 180 days per year with my parents. I left in May of each year and returned after Labor Day in September. My summers were spent with my sister and brother. My sister had married an enlisted man in the Army and my brother was an officer in the Army.

I loved living on Army bases. There was always someone to play with and I got to eat some of the most incredible food at the homes of my "summer friends".

The greatest gift of growing up free without conventional boundaries was I had an opportunity to walk to my own beat. My community wasn't simply limited to a small, rural farm community but it was a collective richness of life experiences. So I never looked up to any single person but rather I looked at communities for my inspiration.

Some people say that it is important for students to have teachers who look like them. But I say it's more important for students to have teachers who empower them. I was academically empowered throughout my K-12 career. Empowered to trust that I had the ability to do the work.

Empowered to question processes and policies when they didn't make sense to me; and, ultimately empowered to study abroad in Australia during my sophomore year of high school. These experiences molded not only how I viewed education but also how I perceived the value of education.

It is also true that teachers teach how they are taught—and this is deeper than just what teachers are taught during their four years of college about education. Every single classroom experience shapes how teachers show up in their own classrooms with their students. For me, because I was empowered, I show up in the classroom in a manner that empowers my students. Some of my students never had an opportunity to make a single academic choice in their life. When I ask the simple question "What do you plan to do after you get your high school diploma?" For many, this is the first time that they have a chance to make a choice about their own academic future.

Emmett

Emmett Alicyn Mabry

Contrary to popular belief and what media sources would make anyone believe, children don't just wake up one day and start lashing out. It also doesn't happen overnight. My story with bullying starts in 2002.

In 2002, I was in K-4 (Pre-K). I was attending a private school, and we all wore uniforms. Everyone had matching everything. You would think there was nothing for anyone to tease anyone about. That wasn't the case. The only thing that wasn't in uniform was our hair. My hair was styled like every other girl's hair in my grade. I wore plaits for most of the school year and braids in the summer. When children wear plaits or braids, it's very common to style them with colorful bows, hair clips, multi-colored beads, and other accessories.

The very instance of bullying that I vividly remember is the day that I stayed with my grandma. My grandma did my hair in plaits as usual, and she put clips at the end of my hair. The clips that she put on the ends of my hair were slightly different than the clips my mom put on the ends of my hair. She had these rectangle-shaped clips, and my mom usually used the butterfly ones. All the other girls also used butterfly clips at the end of their hair. My grandma dropped me off as usual, I got into the classroom, and put my bookbag away. Nothing was unusual. I took my seat and we started our first assignment of the morning. It's then that the girl sitting across from me noticed that I was wearing different clips. She asked me some questions and I answered them. After that, she didn't say anything. We were all quietly doing our work until snack time.

At snack time, she started making comments about my hair clips about how they weren't as pretty. To an adult, that doesn't sound like a big deal but I was 4 years old at the time and my feelings were very hurt. There were several similar incidents like this with this girl throughout the school year, but that one stands out the most. Like any other child, I wanted approval from my peers and wanted to fit in and be like everyone else. I wasn't the only girl in my class that this girl treated this way, but it was still extremely hurtful. As time went on, I told my teachers, the owners of the school, and there was always an excuse. For context, this was a Christian school, and the only consequence for teasing was to formally apologize in front of school administrators, hug it out, ask for forgiveness, and as a last resort they would have to write something like "I won't do [action] again" so many times on a piece of paper.

Nothing serious. I told my mom and grandma about it and the response was something along the lines of "they're jealous," "that's how kids are," and things like that. That made me feel a little better because I knew that there wasn't anything wrong with me, but it still hurt.

At the end of the 2002-2003 school year, my mom asked me if I wanted to go to public school or remain at the Christian academy. I was told that if I went to public school, I could ride the bus and I wouldn't have to wake up as early. That sounded extremely appealing to me as a Kindergartner because I was used to waking up at 5:30-6:00 am to get to school on time. Going to public school meant I got an extra hour of sleep. On TV, they made riding the bus look extremely fun, so I was excited. I was also excited that I wouldn't have to see the girl who teased me in K-4 again.

Right before I started Kindergarten, my parents bought a new house and there were a lot of other kids my age in this neighborhood. I didn't know any of them before I started attending public school. In summer 2003, I remember going to my first open house and meeting my Kindergarten teacher. I absolutely loved her classroom. I was so excited to be in her class. My teacher's teaching assistant knew my family personally because she had worked with my grandma. We also got to meet my bus driver at the open house, and the bus driver was a very sweet person. The school year started off quite warm. I went home happy and excited about the new school year. The fact that we were in a new neighborhood and I didn't know any of the other kids didn't faze me. At our previous residence, there were no other kids near us. It wasn't something I'd paid attention to.

On the first day of school, I got up early. My mom made me cinnamon rolls, did my hair and walked me to the bus stop. I got on the bus and the bus driver told me to find a seat and make sure I remained seated. That sounded like a very simple task, but I quickly learned that that was not a simple task when you were the new kid. There were some kids on the bus already and they wouldn't let me sit with them, so I ended up sitting in the very back with a 5th grader. Although there were no formally assigned seats, children assigned themselves seats and would politely ask you to move if you were in their usual spot. I went to the back of the bus every day, until one day I had fallen asleep and the bus driver missed my stop. When that happened, she asked me why I sat in the back and I told her that the other kids wouldn't let me sit anywhere else. The next day, she formally assigned everyone a seat. Then I had to ride at the front of the bus, which wasn't a bad experience because we all had assigned seats. No one could argue and it was a smooth school year. For privacy reasons, I won't name her, but this bus driver was one of my school heroes because she was the only person who listened and took it seriously the first time. If lunchtime and recess were like that, my academic experience would've been a lot different.

Lunch time in Kindergarten was okay. We had 30 minute lunches so we had to eat fast. There wasn't much time for talking. Sometimes we would joke around, but it was mostly eating.

Recess in Kindergarten started off fun, but by the end of the school year, outside recess became another socialization experience I dreaded in school. It seemed like overnight it went from casual playing tag and seeing who could swing the highest to being pushed off the swings, name calling, and constantly being told I couldn't play somewhere by other children.

What could've sparked this change in behavior? In Kindergarten, I was more academically advanced than my peers but there's no gifted class for Kindergarten. I think some kids were jealous of that and they called me names like "know-it-all" and "weird". These may not sound too terrible to an adult but to a 5 year old, acceptance by peers is so important. When I told the teacher, the response was similar to K-4. "Just ignore it." Eventually, I stopped telling. Sometimes, if it got really bad I would confide in my grandma. Her response was similar to the teachers. My grandma never ignored me, but I think she didn't know what to tell me. She's a Silent Gen, so when she was attending school things were a lot different.

The passive responses to this type of behavior from other children as early as Pre-K enabled their behavior to evolve from mean jokes to assault and battery.

First and second grade were about the same as Kindergarten. Despite all the mean things the kids said to me, I was still nice to everyone. I didn't hold grudges and would share things with kids who were mean to me.

Fast forward to the 2007-2008 school year. This was my 3rd grade school year. The small town I grew up in was expanding and the elementary school was overcrowded. In response, a new school was built. I was the first 3rd grade class at this new school. With the exception of a handful of kids, I was still in the same district as most of the kids I'd been going to school with. I rode the bus with the same kids. It doesn't seem like much should have changed, but a lot changed.

For myself and other kids, there was a lot of anxiety about a new school, new routine and not knowing what this upcoming school year had in store. For the most part, the learning environment was the same but the biggest difference was that this school incorporated more peer to peer interaction. We could pick where we wanted to sit at lunch, even if it wasn't with our class. There was minimal supervision. Overall, there was less staff at this school. The closest we had to supervision was a lunch monitor that occasionally walked around. The teachers could see us from their break room very clearly, but they couldn't hear us. Pre-K and Kindergarten had to share a paraprofessional, while other grades didn't have one at all. This was also my formal introduction to gaslighting.

Before 2007, para-professionals were in all classrooms for all grades within K-5. Having a paraprofessional or any other staff member who was available to consistently monitor all interactions made a huge difference in how students interacted, in a bad way. Another thing that made this school year very different was watching what we now call The Great Recession unfold. The chaos that was going on in many kids' homes because of this economic downturn was following them to school.

The beginning of the school year was awkward but okay because everything was new, but after fall break, things took a turn for the worst. Book fairs, bake sales, donation contests were some of the things that started around fall break. Up to this point, 2007-2008 had been a normal school year for me. Nothing in my home life had changed. My family gave me money for all the festivities that come with Fall and it was the same amount I usually got. I consistently bought the same items every year. I bought a variety pack of baked goods, at least 1 book set, a few toys or accessories that were related to the books. Every year, my grandma usually had enough to spare for the donation contest and my class consistently won the pizza party. This year was no exception.

Before this year, these festivities were things that were considered fun. This turned into something else for kids to negatively say something about. After returning from the book fair and putting my purchases away, one kid asked me what accessories I got and what came with. I happily explained. I was so happy about the books that I wasn't considering accessories. Class quickly resumed right after I put my things away.

I'm still at a point in my life where I am rationalizing the things that I experienced from my point of view as a child. Some of it is still extremely hard to describe but the reason why everything felt so overwhelming growing up was that it really did feel like it was all happening at once. Some of it is childhood and some of it is trauma but the combination of the two distorts the perception of time. The way I recall middle school feels like it all happened within a couple of days, although I know it was much longer than that. It's like when you're experiencing the trauma and it's actively going on, it feels like time is going by very very slowly. Once you're out of here, and you've been able to distance from it/grow from it, then it's like it's all mashed up into a couple of days and some events are mashed into one day even though I know for a fact that they are not just one day or a month, they were definitely long-term events.

I had started thinking about homeschooling when I was in K-4 because I had no problem doing any of my work. I was already ahead of my peers, and I saw it as a distraction from learning. The topic of homeschooling was a weekly conversation because I was so miserable in school. My parent's rebuttal was that I needed socialization. That was the constant rebuttal. When I was younger, I didn't understand their argument. The older I got, the more I disagreed. Once I learned how to write academic papers in 3rd grade, it was over for my parents' rebuttals. Every credible source I found about homeschooling said the exact opposite of what they were saying.

Finally, when things became too much after all the changes I described before in my school, it was truly time for the big step. I'm glad my mother was right there to help me through all the stages of it, including the decision for dual enrollment. It has been challenging but it also has been a blessing. Most importantly, it has been the kind of hard work that leads somewhere, that opens doors, and takes you out of the underground tunnel into the open sky, so you can make your future the way you want it to be.

Thank you, mom. Thanks for not just helping me but countless others who needed help just like I did.

Niles

Niles Mabry

I don't remember a lot about going to public school other than having a few friends there. I just know that I always felt like I was somewhat behind in my classes.

I learned that if I was quiet sometimes teachers wouldn't call on me to answer questions. Answering the questions was hard because sometimes I didn't really understand what I had read or what the question was asking.

My mom was working a lot of hours at the University because she was a Dean. So she told me I had to go to Mrs. Lawson's class after school and Mrs. Lawson would help me with my homework. Mrs. Lawson was the Kindergarten teacher and she was nice. I think that was the first time I made a friend.
But honestly public school is a blur to me because I spent so much time feeling lost.

When my mom told me that I was going to be homeschooled, I was happy at first because I was going to be able to learn at my own pace. But I also knew that I was really behind in math because I didn't understand multiplying at all and reading was hard. I tried my best in public school to keep up but the harder I tried to keep up the more I fell behind.

When I started homeschooling though, that all changed. My mom hired Mrs. Devorah who really helped me with my reading. She also helped me with my writing too because the way she taught me reading and writing, it made sense.

My mom knew if I didn't have somewhere to go that I wouldn't come out of my room, so she made sure that we were at a different homeschool co-op every day. My favorite homeschool cooperative classes were culinary arts and a geopolitical class. I am graduating this year and I'm not sure what I want to do next.

That makes me a little nervous but my mom enrolled me in some Google certification classes to learn how to support businesses with managing their Adwords accounts. I am also taking driving lessons and I will get my driver's license this summer.

I may not have big plans as yet of what I want to be ten years from now, but I know the difference between having the luxury to plan one's future and not having one at all.

Beginnings

Dr. Annise Mabry

For years, my daughter begged me to homeschool her; and, time and again, I found a reason for why it wasn't a good idea. My reluctance allowed her to fall victim to what was called by our school superintendent at the time "one of the most extreme cases" of bullying ever experienced in our county. I still carry the guilt to this day.

The bullies got bolder; they stabbed her with pencils, hit her in the back of the head with literature books, and spat in her food at lunch. Her only safe place to eat was the bathroom. Each time she tried to report the assaults, she was told the administration couldn't do anything because they didn't actually see it happen. But the bullies didn't stop with just the physical assaults—soon, they began taunting her on social media as well.

My daughter's spirit broke. She became angry at everything and everyone. The tipping point came when my daughter—who had never been in trouble in her life—was suspended three times in a thirty- day period. My background training saw the escalation of her anger with each suspension—and the truth is, I was angry too. I had done everything that I was trained to do as an educator and as a law enforcement official, but it wasn't enough to save my own child.

When I asked for the opportunity to use the hospital homebound services for the remaining sixty days of the school year, I was told by the county educational services coordinator, "Hospital homebound services are for medically fragile children only. I cannot waste those resources on a child that is not medically fragile."

I was dumbfounded. However I pushed, and she was granted a good teacher for her homebound period. But the reality was that the intervention came too late. My daughter was traumatized; she still carries those emotional scars to this day. My greatest regret is that I left her in that toxic environment for five months. At last I decided it was time to homeschool.

I had no idea how I would juggle the demands of my full-time career with those of homeschooling, but I was determined to figure it out.

I needed a curriculum that would be easy on me as a parent. But I didn't resist my daughter's suggestion of using K12. As it turned out, it was a huge burden on both of us. It was repetitive, the online teachers had no idea how to make content engaging, and despite the hardest of effort, my daughter still failed end-of-the-year eighth grade test.

Things became easier when I discovered that in Georgia, I was legally allowed to award my daughter a high school diploma through homeschooling. I also found out that it was okay for me to choose my own curriculums for every subject-matter, and even switch them mid-way if problems arose. Similarly, it was also legal to hire tutors for content I didn't wish to teach myself.

I was busy swinging between the mental health and academic ups and downs of my daughter, when I discovered that the public schooling system was now failing my young son as well. He had never been allowed to work on his below-grade reading and math skills, and now in 4th grade he was suddenly being expected to perform above and beyond.

The day I told my son I was going to homeschool him as well, he let out a big whoop of joy. By working my way through specialized math and reading programs and hiring expert teachers to teach them, I was able to create learning opportunities for my son which worked. Both his math and reading have significantly improved, and it fills me with joy and pride to see him work independently for the first time in his life.

After my daughter graduated, my neighbors' daughter, who was also a high-school dropout, became interested and I agreed to help her. I soon realized that she only needed four classes to graduate.

When she finished her last class, her mom threw her a graduation party. People in the community who had been watching our journey also professed their desire to homeschool and they wanted my help to issue their own homeschool high school diplomas. That's how the idea of Tiers Free Academy was born.

The Navigators

Dr. Annise Mabry

After working with my neighbor's daughter, I knew what I wanted in a curriculum. I wanted it to provide a pre-assessment and to be entirely online. I also needed the curriculum to automatically move the student up or down, based on their current performance level. This way, the student would never feel overwhelmed and would master the content at their own pace. Once I acquired the curriculum that fit my specifications, I needed to test it on a student who was not a recent dropout. So I reached out to my sister-in-law Helen.

Helen had dropped out of school before she reached high school and for years, she had talked about getting her high school diploma. She had taken every GED class that she could and, no matter how hard she studied, she couldn't pass the test. This made her my ideal curriculum tester.

So I told Helen that I wanted to build an alternative path to a high school diploma by using the homeschool laws. These laws empowered parents to issue their own diplomas to their children, but were not known well-enough to be utilized more commonly. Helen gave me all the confirmation that I needed. I told her I really believed it could work, and without hesitation she promised she would help me to test it to make sure it did. Helen used to say she was going to be my hype person. For what felt like months, I sent Helen links to online curricula that I thought were brilliant and she would send them back to me with a simple note: "This won't work."

One day she said, "You are making the same mistake all those other programs made. You are trying to build this like an educator. Don't do this program like an educator! Think about all of the things that stop people from getting an education."

So I threw out all of the online curricula that I had optioned and started over. First, I did a search for online credit recovery classes. I found two providers, and I did exactly what Helen said to do: stop thinking like an educator. I didn't research the curriculum—that honestly didn't matter. I needed a curriculum that would fit the needs of my students, not the other way around. At last I found two providers that could serve the right solution.

I contacted both and explained what I was trying to do. Both gave me a thirty-day trial, so I enrolled Helen in both programs. Helen got frustrated with the first program immediately. Their videos were either too long in some topic areas or didn't explain concepts well enough in others. Helen liked the Acellus program the best. So, that was what I selected as our curriculum provider for Tiers Free Academy.

Most educators when they are designing a program tend to go into the box with other educators as their sounding boards. I was guilty of this but Helen's words always ring in my head when I think of implementing new things into Tiers Free— "Don't do this program like an educator! Think about all of the things that stop people from getting an education."

With that being said, this program isn't easy. Students do one class every 30 days and getting exceptions for additional days is an exception—not a norm. The lesson that I am teaching them by standing firm in the 30-day deadline is 'life is always going to happen to you but you have to maintain your focus no matter what'.

By now, word was getting out into the community that I was teaching parents how to issue a legal, homeschool diploma. I was quickly gaining the reputation as the homeschool expert in our community. Just as I was expecting to get happily busier with what I now believed to be my life's true calling ... came Helen's diagnosis: she had Stage 4 lung cancer and less than a year to live.

I wanted to spend Helen's last year doing a bucket list of places to visit, but all she wanted to do with her precious time was to help me design the curriculum and finish her classes. It took me a long time to realize that graduating was the last item on Helen's bucket list.

Even with Stage 4 lung cancer, she logged into her classes and she worked. She worked when she felt like it and many times when I know she didn't. Helen finished all of her classes and said to me, "I want a full graduation ceremony. Students need a graduation ceremony. It's a rite of passage." By now, I had seven families who had enrolled in Tiers Free Academy. Helen was right. We started planning a graduation ceremony for May 2017.

Helen got sicker and this ceremony became more than just ceremony—it became our last dance. We finalized the graduation details and selected the school colors of black and silver. Helen was adamant about the graduation style and colors.

She said, "Graduations have to be elegant. Black and silver are elegant."

Our last conversation before she entered hospice was about her gown. She wanted me to make sure it wasn't "that shiny metallic-looking material." I promised it wouldn't be.

Helen passed away before I could hold the May 2017 ceremony, but we made sure to have an empty chair in her honor. Her sister accepted her diploma.

Helen's death became the northern star in my navigation of this new academic landscape. I now knew how to determine a student's academic readiness for a program like mine. Just because a person didn't have any experience taking high school classes didn't mean they weren't academically ready for the journey.

This insight too had come from Helen. As she had explained, the most frustrating things about adult literacy programs was they all assumed she couldn't comprehend high school-level work due to her lack of high-school exposure. She made me promise to never put students in an environment where they felt like they couldn't win.

Even today, when I find myself stuck on a student's academic path,, I sometimes ask, "What would Helen need to succeed?"

The hardest thing my students have to do is to say, "I want my diploma." Those four words throw them into a time warp to a place of academic failure. These students were embarking on a journey back into academic pain. My job was to transform their most painful moments into their greatest success. I had to be strategic with helping them achieve academic wins. They needed both short-term and long-term wins on this path to keep motivated.

THE TIERS FREE STORIES

Parent's Story
Crystal Spence

Mother of 2018 Graduate

Tiers Free Academy Alternative Diploma Program

My daughter was in the 11th grade and struggling at the time with the public school system. She had given up and was going to drop out with her only option to get a diploma being the GED at the adult literacy program. As I stood feeling helpless and venting to Dr. Mabry (or Doc as she's known in our family), she enlightened me on the option of homeschooling. This would have allowed my daughter to obtain an actual High School Diploma. I didn't know a lot about homeschooling but it seemed like it would be complicated and it didn't seem feasible for us at the time. But that's where we learned about the Tiers Free Academy Alternative Diploma Program.

My daughter was nervous about doing school again at first because of her experience with the public school and another local alternative high school program. Public school began to fail my daughter as early as middle school. The classrooms were run by the students rather than the teachers. She was bullied to the point she began to struggle academically. It all ended up impacting her emotional health and she fell into depression.

In the past I had tried local programs. For instance, there was one which cost us $75 a week. The only thing that my child got from there was unhealthy relationships with other unmotivated students who were as lost as she was. The other program seemed to be in place for the money more than the education and that ultimately failed my child too.

When we finally decided to enroll with Dr. Mabry's program, we noticed differences right away. The biggest difference was that we had a lot of flexibility with the curriculum and it wasn't a 'one size fits all' approach. I watched my daughter's self-confidence soar as she finished her class each month. Even though all of the classes were online and she never physically sat in the classroom, Dr. Mabry was there with her every step of the way.

Her graduation day was the best part. I watched with my family as she received her high school diploma. It was presented to her in full cap and gown which was groundbreaking for her self-esteem! This was the best news and immediately her life-altering journey began!

For other parents who find themselves in a similar situation, please step outside of your comfort zone and know that your child does not have to go through all the unnecessary stress destroying their

self-confidence. Homeschool students can receive a real life education without suffering the frustrations and inequalities of the public system. Homeschooling is not only equivalent to the standard public school education, it's flexible enough to be fun and effective enough to create a solid foundation enabling your child to thrive.

Using a program like Tiers Free Academy sends your child a few key messages they need in life. Not only does their family believe in them and their ability to succeed, but also that you all are refusing to settle for only a GED. These children are ripe and ready to receive the skills and mental acuity a fair education can offer and they deserve nothing less.

Dr. Annise Mabry saw a real need in our communities. Providing a scaffolding to the students who have no support in the public system, her academy can break through the educational barrier. It's the barrier that ultimately becomes an employment barrier and creates a vicious cycle of failure and crime. She is breaking that cycle each time she helps a high school dropout transform into a high school graduate. She is a quiet storm sending a real message by her actions to families and communities. Homes where students have given up on school and communities where leaders are ready to make real economic change... they don't have to settle for academic programs that don't fit their needs or GED programs that have their own stigma.

#EducationIsPower

Graduate Story - I
Jessica Stephens

Class of 2020 Graduate

Tiers Free Academy

Reflection Speech

Wow! My journey through school has been a very different experience. Let me explain that a little more, so you all will have a better understanding.

When I was in elementary school, I remember I would get in trouble every single week for either talking too much or not paying attention. When I was in fourth grade, my mother took me to the doctor for a check up because she believed I had hearing problems. She said I talked very loud all the time. Imagine that. I ended up getting my adenoids taken out and when I went to school the following year, my behavior was still bad but my grades improved!

The truth is when I went to school, I was just releasing the frustrations that I was experiencing at home. At home, I was being sexually abused. I was placed into foster care when I was in the 6th grade but when we went to court and everything was finalized, I was sent back home.

My behavior was really bad in school and I got expelled during both my 6th and 7th grade years. My 8th grade year, I was homeschooled online but I never attended because I didn't have any drive to do my school work. I was on an ankle monitor and probation at this point. I ended up informing my probation officer of the abuse and she took me out of the home that day. I was placed back into foster care. I was sent to a residential program in Bowdon, Ga (Carroll County) called Kids Peace. I completed my 8th grade year there. The staff and the teachers I had there really made me feel like I was part of a family, so everything improved with me. My behavior, my grades, everything about me changed.

I decided that I wanted to live with my dad at the beginning of my 9th grade year, so I transitioned into my dad's home. But I hadn't ever dealt with the trauma I had endured as a kid so I started acting out again. I started skipping school and making very poor choices. I ended up stealing the janitor's phone at school and got caught.

The trouble I was causing my dad and grandmother was just too much to endure at the time, so I was back on the road to go to another residential treatment facility. My 10th grade year started at Anne Elizabeth Shepherd Home for girls in Columbus, Ga. Again I started to feel like I was part of a family and grew strong bonds with the staff there. They all gave me that mother feeling and sensitivity that I was longing for. I went to school on the campus and I was making almost all Straight As . When I would go to my cottage dorm area at night, the only thing that made me happy was learning. So I studied every single night. It was so fun to me and gave me hope in my life. In the middle of my 10th grade year, I graduated parts of the program and I was able to attend public school. I went to Northside High school in

Columbus, GA but due to some issues of confidentiality and treatment, I was pulled from school and started my 11th grade year back at Anne Elizabeth Shepherd Home for girls. A few months later they ended up placing me back in the public school.

Keep in mind that as I am bouncing around from school district to school district, I am losing my high school credits in the process. Either I'm retaking classes that I finished or I'm not being placed into classes that I needed, because each school had their own registration system and none of the systems were connected. All of these credit transfers are creating a big mess.

So I ended up skipping school and making poor choices once again.

The Home did an emergency transfer for me to go to another group home. So in the middle of my 11th grade year, I was now at a group home called Arabella in Waverly Hall, GA.

Arabella was very small and only had about 10 girls living there. It was different for me because I was used to homes with 100 or more girls. I was still continuing to make straight As and Bs the whole 11th grade year. A year later I was transitioning out into a foster home. This lady was my CASA worker through the Department of Family and Children Services (DFCS). So I did the beginning of my 12th grade year at Centennial High school in Roswell, GA, but she kicked me out of her house at 7 am on my 18th birthday.

I went to my dad's house for a few weeks while DFCS was trying to find me somewhere to go. Since now I was 18, placement was very limited for me. I ended up getting my own apartment through an Independent Living Program (ILP) through DFCS. I was still in my senior year when I got transferred to Alonzo A. Crim Open Campus High School in Atlanta.

My credits were so messed up and I was in a credit recovery program.

Thus, even though my GPA was above 3.5, I would not be allowed to graduate as a valedictorian.

This was the first time that I had all online classes and that made things very difficult. I ended up dropping out with 2 credits left. I was basically kicked out of DFCS and lost my apartment.

I was homeless with no high school diploma so I jumped into the streets and never had any time to go back to school. School was always kind of a thought in the back of my mind but it didn't matter anymore to me.

I got arrested a few times and had babies back to back. My last time in jail, I was informed of a program that could greatly improve my life. I met Kasey McClure, went into the 4sarah program and was reunited with my kids. I was given an opportunity to go back to school at the age of 22.

4Sarah is a non-profit for women and girls in a position like me. It helped me to get enrolled in the Tiers Free Academy Program. I was enrolled in the online classes through Dr. Mabry. At first it was a bit difficult so I asked Dr. Mabry for help. When I talked to Dr. Mabry for the first time, I was so amazed. She was believing in me more than I believed in myself. She believed that I was going to finish the program and I would graduate with my high school diploma.

I remember feeling amazed that she talked to me for a whole hour! For the first time in a long time, I started to dream about my future and not my life in the present. I was telling her I wanted to be in law enforcement and - wow - to my surprise, this woman instantly started to help me carve out my roadmap for exactly that future.

A few weeks after that talking with Dr. Mabry, I started to do the school work that was required. I stayed up all night doing my school work. I would wake up to my baby girls and then go to work.

I was tired but I stuck with it every day and finally I completed my classes! I remember the feeling I had and I just looked at my baby girls sleeping in their beds and I cried. I was so happy. I finally did it! Now I am looking for colleges and I really am happy that I know that a career choice for me is not impossible!

For the first time in a long time, I have hope. Now that's something I have never had even when I was a child.

Thrive with Pride - I
Brandilyn Cromer

Class of 2019 Graduate

Macon County Chiefs' Diploma Program

Thrive with Pride Scholarship Recipient

My struggles with traditional schooling started when I came out as bisexual. I was going to school in a small town and people in traditional schooling weren't very accepting of my sexual orientation and yes, I got bullied—a lot.

But it wasn't the bullying that made me quit school. It was when a girl who I had been dating accused me of raping her because her grandmother found out that she was attracted to women. Her grandmother didn't approve of same-sex relationships. That girl didn't want to risk ruining her relationship with her grandmother, so she ruined my reputation at school instead.

So not only was I being bullied for being bisexual, I also acquired the reputation of being that girl who forced herself onto other girls. It is no surprise then that I was extremely isolated.

Thank goodness I still had sports. Sports were my lifeline and kept me grounded. But then I got injured and had to have knee surgery.

While I was out of school recovering from knee surgery, the rumors started again and now the only outlet that I had in playing sports was gone. I was overwhelmed. I was tired of fighting the rumors so I just quit school.

It was a decision that weighed heavily on my entire family—especially my mom and my grandfather.

When I learned about the Macon County Chief's Diploma Program from Chief Hart's post on Facebook, I called her to see if the program was legit and she said yes. Orientation for the program was on a cold, rainy Saturday morning and honestly all I wanted to do was sleep. Chief Hart called and said she was coming to pick me up to make sure that I didn't miss signing up.

Accepting that ride from Chief Hart changed my life. This program actually gave me a chance to receive my high school diploma rather than my GED. When I learned that this program had the support of the Atlanta Pride Committee, I realized that I could apply to receive a Thrive with Pride Scholarship here. It was the first time that I discovered that scholarship money existed for something besides sports.

I was even more excited when I found out that I had been selected as the first rural Georgia Thrive with Pride Scholarship recipient. Receiving the Thrive with Pride Scholarship really showed me that people actually cared about me and an entire community of people who I never met loved me. The Thrive with Pride Scholarship gave me the boost that I needed to finish the program.

My advice to others would be to go through this program, get your diploma and move forward with your life. Since I've received my diploma, I'm working on finishing my Certified

Nursing Assistant (CNA) license, then I'll be going back for my Licensed Practical Nurse (LPN) and hopefully bridge over to a Registered Nurse (RN). Life has been great since I've received my diploma.

Police Story - I
Chief Rachael Lee Hart

Oglethorpe Police

Department Oglethorpe, GA

I've grown up in Macon County, GA. My grandparents owned several businesses in Montezuma, GA so this is home for me. I started my law enforcement career in 2013 and I became Chief of Police with the Oglethorpe Police Department in 2017.

Oglethorpe GA is a small, tight close knit farming community in Southwest GA. We have one traffic light and our largest retail store is Dollar General. We are located about an hour away from Warner Robins, GA and about 45 minutes away from Albany, GA. Our largest local employer is International Paper.

I think sometime around 2016, the tensions between the community and the police department had been simmering and on the night I'm describing today, they reached a boiling point. What started out as a routine disorderly conduct call quickly escalated. Citizens began to come into the streets. They picked up whatever objects they could find to throw at the officers and the patrol cars. I was hit in the face with a rock.

The most important take-away from that night was not a single officer used force. But there were some deep emotional wounds inflicted within the public and the policing communities. I promised myself on that night that if I ever had the opportunity to become the Chief, I would work with the community to heal these wounds.

One year later, my Chief died and I found myself in that role. We had five known national street gangs operating within 2.1 square miles and there was still a lot of tension between the police department and the community. Citizens saw the police as a gang. The officers felt they were patrolling outnumbered, outmaneuvered, and ill-equipped. I couldn't change the residents in the community so I knew I needed to shift how we as a law enforcement agency responded to the community. The police department needed a shift in the dynamics from a reactive response to a proactive approach.

I wanted to bring community policing to our department and I tried everything that I knew but I was limited with resources and officers.

Then one day, my agency was invited to participate in a Community Policing Pilot program that was being designed for small rural law enforcement agencies with 10 or fewer full time officers. The first two programs being rolled out were Christmas with a Cop and the Macon County Chief's Diploma Program.

The Macon County Chiefs' Diploma Program is a program under the Tiers Free Academy Homeschool Cooperative. It allows a law enforcement agency to partner with the homeschool cooperative to reduce recidivism in their community by providing adults 18 and over the opportunity to earn a high school diploma.

Most parents don't realize that they aren't left to the mercy of adult literacy programs if their child is unable to graduate from high school. GA law clearly states that as long as the parent or guardian files a GA Declaration of Intent to Homeschool with the GA Department of Education and provides (or hires a tutor to provide) academic instruction in math, reading, science, and social studies for 4.5 hours per day that the parent has the right to issue their own homeschool diploma.

Homeschool graduates are entitled to all of the same privileges and rights as a public school student in the state of Georgia as it relates to attending college, enlisting in the military, and obtaining employment.

I knew we had a few adults who didn't have high school diplomas but I had no idea how many. One day we were getting set up for municipal court and people were coming in to report for probation. I decided to see how many people had a high school diploma. As I began talking to people, I learned that 8 out of 10 people on probation didn't have a high school diploma. Most of them were over the age of 25.

When I got this '8 out of 10' figure, I was shocked. I realized why it was hard for people to get jobs. Some in leadership felt that people weren't getting jobs because they weren't looking. But the truth was they were looking and applying but they didn't have a high school diploma which is a minimum entry requirement for all of the jobs posted.

This program has changed not only my agency but also my community. Our officers are taking citizens' applications to enroll in the program and they stop by the houses of our program participants when they are on patrol just to check in to see how classes are going. Since 2019, 99 adults in the Macon County area have graduated with their high school diploma. We have graduates who are attending South Georgia Technical College and Central Georgia Technical College.

We (myself included) never realized the full economic impact of how having a large number of your working age population without a high school diploma strained all of the other social service systems in the community. Until we got involved in the pilot program, I never knew that a child with one parent who didn't graduate from high school only has a 30% chance of becoming a high school graduate. If that child has two parents who didn't finish high school, there is a 70% likelihood that the child won't become a high school graduate. This program changed my community because it went to the root cause of generational illiteracy.

Graduate Story - II
Rachel Wall

Class of 2021 Graduate

Box Breakers Program

As a child going through school was very difficult. Between trying to complete my work with zero at-home assistance, social obstacles, and bullying I just couldn't persevere through all of it. Concentrating on studies and simply getting through a school day while living in a very toxic home environment wasn't an easy task to say the least.

I attempted to get my GED about a year before I started the alternative diploma program. I went to a local college campus to take their pre-test. I never heard back from them with my results which discouraged me from continuing to try. I had a very hard time finding information and lacked the self-confidence I needed to move through the process on my own without any guidance. The obstacles of trying to figure out the cost and my conviction that I just wasn't smart enough to start, much less complete, my GED led to me giving up at first.

An amazing friend of mine named Heidi Cloud learned about the program and did everything she could to set me up with Dr. Mabry. Once I started my lessons, my confidence improved with every class I completed; but without Heidi helping me take those first steps I wouldn't be here today.

The biggest difference about the diploma program was that I was able to pick my classes and complete them at my own pace. Although the program had deadlines for classes, I was able to set my own goals and meet them. The design of the program was amazing as well. The classes were designed to quiz and test after every step to make sure I understood instead of just failing me if I missed something and leaving me unsure of exactly where I went wrong. If I didn't understand a concept right away the program reviews made sure I was on-pace instead of allowing me to move through without that understanding.

The most amazing part of this journey was that moment I found out I received a scholarship because of my performance. I was over the moon. The idea that people I didn't know had recognized my achievements and wanted to help me complete the program was honestly life changing.

Since the beginning of finding the alternative diploma program everyone has shown me a level of kindness, I have never received in my past. I can see how people associated with this program are taking time out of their lives to help me complete my education. Having that financial stress off my back completely changed my perspective on what I was able to accomplish and was a tremendous help to me in continuing the path to my goals.

But I'm not going to stop at my high school diploma. I have applied to the University of North Georgia. I hope to study General Science and receive my A.S. degree. I chose the University of North Georgia because they're the perfect match for me financially, as well as the fact that they offer mostly online courses. The ability to continue my education while still able to be home with my family is ideal.

Graduate Story - III
Kateisha Smith

Class of 2020 Graduate

Macon County Chiefs' Diploma Program

I learned about the Macon County Chief's Diploma Program on social media. At first, I didn't believe the program was real until I saw it first-hand. As I watched the Class of 2019 graduate and then get accepted into colleges, I wanted to get my diploma too. I was so excited! I called Dr. Mabry and asked her to sign me up.

I struggled in the traditional education system not because I couldn't do the work but because I wasn't focused and didn't want to do the work. I had teachers who cared about me but they didn't know how to connect with me or how to motivate me. Then my grandmother got sick so I was having to take a few days off to help my mom take care of her. A few days became a week and a week became a month. When I had missed too many days, I just dropped out of school.

I started attending the South GA Technical College GED classes after dropping out. I took the GED test and failed it so many times that I gave up. Honestly, I thought the Chief's Diploma Program was going to be just like the GED program but it wasn't. I tried to quit the Chief's Diploma Program many a times as well as I wasn't used to working hard for school anymore. But Dr. Mabry wouldn't let me.

I remember the time when I had fallen behind in my class because my mom had gotten sick and I was giving up. Dr. Mabry sent an officer from the police department to ask me what time I was going to be logging into my class for the day. When I explained that I was going to take a break because my mom was sick, Dr. Mabry said "I'm sorry to hear that but when are you going to finish your work?"

I learned a lot more that day than just what was in the class. This program forever changed not only my life but my family's life too.

Dr. Mabry was firm and tough. She tells all of us: "The only thing I give you is 30 days to complete a class. You are going to earn every letter on your diploma that says High School Graduate". I remember the day that I finished my last class. I had finally earned my high school diploma. I hadn't even logged off the computer yet and Dr. Mabry sent me the application link for South GA Technical College. She said there were no breaks in education from this day forward. And she's right. Next year, I am graduating with my Associate's Degree in Education and I am already looking at attending Georgia Southwestern University.

This program has changed my life forever. In 2005, I was a high school dropout. In 2020, I became a high school graduate and a college student. In 2022, I will be a college graduate and enrolling into my Bachelor's program at the university. My life will never be the same because of one social media post and one program that gives people who don't have a high school diploma a second chance.

Police Story - II
Chief Patricia Barber

Marshallville Police Department

Marshallville, GA

I started my law enforcement career in 1986 in Tift County, GA. I was the first African American female to be hired by the Sheriff's Office to first work as a dispatcher and then as a jailer. I became a POST Certified Peace Officer in 1990 and I hit another milestone first—as the first African American female investigator for the Sumter County Sheriff's Office.

Law enforcement isn't just a job to me. It's a calling to serve my community. I was initially hired to work as a part time patrol officer in Marshallville in 2014 and I fell in love with the community. I became the Chief of the Marshallville Police Department in 2019.

Marshallville GA is located in Macon County. People always confuse Macon County with Macon, GA and while the names are the same, the communities are vastly different. Macon County Georgia is a rural farming community and we have one grocery store.

I knew the area because I had worked at the Peach County Sheriff's Office since 1994. What most people don't know about Peach County is that it was formed from parts of Macon County in 1924. So when I began working in Peach County, I met people who remembered when Peach County was part of Macon County.

Macon County is a land rich community and its proximity to Interstate 75 South makes it perfect for people who want to take life a little slower but still have the conveniences of a big city.

Dr. Annise Mabry is my younger sister and when she started the homeschool diploma program to help her daughter graduate from high school, that was the first time that I honestly realized two things. One, that a parent could issue their own homeschool high school diploma.

Two, that a homeschool high school diploma was a valid, legal document that was accepted by colleges, the military, and employers.

I have been serving on the Tiers Free Academy Graduation Committee since 2017. The first time I saw a link to a report from the Georgia Budget and Policy Institute about the number of adults in Georgia without a high school diploma I dropped my phone.

38% of adults 18-24 in Macon County, Georgia didn't have a high school diploma.

Even though I had this information, I wasn't sure what to do with it because I was only a part-time officer who worked four days a month. I knew any real change was going to take a collaborative county-wide effort. I also knew that if anyone could lead such an effort, it was my sister. From the beginning, I knew in my heart that she was going to make it happen.

I knew Dr. Mabry had written a comprehensive community policing model as part of her graduate program coursework, because she made everyone in the family her unpaid editorial staff and we all read her papers. Even though I didn't understand a lot of her statistical analysis, I knew that there was a connection between a high dropout rate and the crime rate. I'd been in law enforcement long enough to know that we weren't simply going to be able to arrest and to patrol our way out of this crisis. We were going to have to do something that had never been done before if we were going to change the direction of an entire generation.

So when Dr. Mabry approached me about bringing a pilot Chief's Diploma Program to Macon County, my response was a resounding YES. I advised her in detail about how my agency could help to make the pilot program a success so it has a chance to become an integral part of the community.

One of the challenges of operating a smaller rural police department is staffing. We frequently work one officer per shift and shifts are covered by part time officers. The part time officers that work at the Marshallville Police Department are here because they genuinely love the community. The challenge of being a part time officer was they often struggled to find a way to build a real relationship with the community.

When I told my officers that we were going to participate in a pilot diploma program for adults, they all looked at me like I was an alien. Honestly, had I not seen the program in action, I would have doubted the impact too.

"Let's just try the program through one graduation cycle," I said and they agreed. But what happened in that one graduation cycle changed my agency.

Three graduation cycles later, this program has changed how my officers interact with the community. I have one officer who even talks about this program to people in his city and has sent four people from his city who needed a high school diploma to enroll in the Macon County Chiefs' Diploma Program.

Dr. Mabry and I started community policing in Marshallville in 2017 with Christmas with a Cop. But even then Dr. Mabry realized that real change in this community was going to take something bigger than passing out toys at Christmas. This program is that 'something bigger'. I have citizens in my community who are grandparents and are receiving their high school diplomas. I have parents who, because now they have a diploma, are enrolling at the technical college and getting industry level certifications. This program has changed my community because it attacks the problems that we encounter not at a "here, let me send you to a program that will pay your past due bill" level but a "let me fix why you are struggling to get employed so you can pay your own bills level".

Graduate Story - IV
Mazie Harris

Class of 2021 Graduate

Macon County Chief's Diploma Program

My cousin Jerry Haugabook told me about the Macon County Chief's Diploma Program. I remember feeling excited because I was finally going to have an opportunity to become a highschool graduate. I was also motivated because I knew that my cousin had graduated from the program and I wanted that same opportunity.

I struggled with attendance when I was in school because I had a baby at a young age. I stopped going to school because I didn't have anyone to help me with my baby so I dropped out.

I tried to get my GED a few times in the past and I even went to classes but I just didn't have a good support system to help me stay focused or motivated.

The biggest difference about this program was that because the classes were online, I was able to keep working while I was taking my classes. Another thing that helped me with the way this program was set up was that I only had one class at a time so it was easier to focus. Also, knowing that I had to finish the class in 30 days made me push myself even harder. This program helped me develop my study habits too because I had to study for each unit test and quiz so I wasn't trying to remember everything for one big test at the end.

This program wasn't easy but it gave me a second chance to become a high school graduate. I want to tell other students who might be struggling in their online classes right now to never give up. It's never too late to get your high school diploma. If this is something you really want and need to better yourself in the future, then you have to stay focused.

My plans now that I am graduating with my high school diploma are to enroll in the nursing program at South Georgia Technical College to become a Licensed Practical Nurse (LPN). I learned a lot more that day than just what was in the class. This program forever changed not only my life but my family's life too.

Dr. Mabry was firm and tough. She tells all of us: "The only thing I give you is 30 days to complete a class. You are going to earn every letter on your diploma that says High School Graduate". I remember the day that I finished my last class. I had finally earned my high school diploma. I hadn't even logged off the computer yet and Dr. Mabry sent me the application link for South GA Technical College. She said there were no breaks in education from this day forward. And she's right. Next year, I am graduating with my Associate's Degree in Education and I am already looking at attending Georgia Southwestern University.

This program has changed my life forever. In 2005, I was a high school dropout. In 2020, I became a high school graduate and a college student. In 2022, I will be a college graduate and enrolling into my Bachelor's program at the university. My life will never be the same because of one social media post and one program that gives people who don't have a high school diploma a second chance.

Thrive with Pride - II
Jerry Haugabook

Class of 2019 Graduate

Macon County Chiefs' Diploma Program

I learned about the Tiers Free Academy, Macon County Chiefs' Diploma Program from my mom and Chief Hart at the Oglethorpe Police Department. My Mom was doing her morning walk one Saturday on the track at the city park and she came home to tell me about this program. She said that Chief Hart and a lady from Atlanta named Dr.

Mabry were doing a program in Oglethorpe at the gym for adults to get their high school diploma. Honestly, I was afraid to go talk to them at first because it didn't seem real. But I decided to turn my fear into faith and went. I signed up the same day.

I had a hard time in high school and I was bullied because of my sexual orientation. I lost focus a lot of the time because I was always fighting. I was always having to fight just to be respected for being myself. My behavior earned me a label as a trouble maker and that label caused me to be placed in a special education learning class for students with behavior disorders.

I didn't have a behavior disorder problem. I was treated as a problem student but I was really the victim of bullying that was never addressed. When I learned that I was going to receive a

Special Education Diploma instead of a high school diploma, I dropped out of school.

I think a lot of my fear was because I had tried to get my GED and no matter how hard I tried, I still couldn't get it. I was tired of trying to make the GED classes fit into my life only to fail one or more subjects of the test.

I didn't believe it at first but the Tiers Free program was different from all the others. I could work and still be able to do all my assignments. I pushed myself a lot to get my work done and it also helped that I had Dr. Mabry as my teacher. Dr. Mabry cared a lot about me and she made sure that I was able to get the work done to graduate on time.

It's no secret in the community that Dr. Mabry's online classes are hard but she doesn't make them so hard that it's impossible to pass. It's just that you have to be focused to finish the class and she's strict about finishing one class every 30 days. She says "The only thing I'm giving you is 30 days to finish a class. You are going to earn every single letter on your diploma that says High School Graduate."

That Saturday morning changed my life forever. I know I'm not the only one who feels this way about how having the Macon County Chiefs' Diploma Program has not only changed lives but it has changed our community too.

To the other adults in the world who are like me, I want to encourage you to keep the faith. The road may seem hard and long. Trust the process and believe in yourself. It's ok to ask for help when you need it, even if it means saying "I need help to get my high school diploma." There's a bright light at the end of what feels like an impossible journey. What got me through those hard days was this Bible verse: Matthew 19:26 "With God all things are possible." You will also find something to keep you going. When someone is there to show you the way, all you have to do is trust and gear up to do the work.

Graduate Story - V
Toronica Price

Class of 2019 Graduate

Tiers Free Academy

My older sister told me about a program coming to Newnan that would help me to get my high school diploma. It didn't seem real at first but I decided to go to the orientation session anyway. When I got there, I didn't see any other cars in the parking lot and I almost told my husband that we were going to turn around.

But he made me go inside and that was the best decision that I made.

School had never really been an easy thing for me. I was having problems in my family and no one in the school system wanted to help. So they put me in special education classes and made me ride a special Ed bus.

I stopped going to school when I got pregnant at 16 and they told me I was going to be too old when I finished school. I tried to go back after I had my baby but the principal of the high school said I was not able to attend that school and sent me to the GED program. I tried for several years to get my GED and I would always come close to passing the test but miss it by a few points.

I think that is probably why I wasn't really confident in the diploma program because it was online and I thought I was going to be alone at home in a class with no help. I was wrong. The online classes weren't easy but the online classroom was user friendly. I honestly think I got more help in the online class than I ever got in the classroom. Dr. Mabry was always a text message away when I needed help.

When I graduated with my high school diploma, I immediately enrolled into the Early Childhood Education program at West Central Technical College and began working on my Associate's Degree. Two years later, I'm getting ready to take my GACE (Georgia Assessments for the Certification of Educators) test to start working on my Bachelor's Degree.

Being the only person to show up for that orientation session that Saturday afternoon changed my life. My daughter is now enrolled in this program and I am so proud of her. The sky is the limit with this program.

Graduate Story - VI
Stephanie Johnson

Class of 2021

Tiers Free Academy

Growing up, school was very challenging in the first few years of elementary school because I was dealing with bullying from my peers at school. I was bullied for my moles which resulted in me not feeling confident. I also experienced some trauma from a family member. My grandfather sexually assaulted me, which resulted in me, an all honor roll student to get F's. But I moved past that era by taking therapy and confiding in my mom and sister. I also made friends who went through similar experiences, so we healed together by talking through our feelings. As my childhood school years are coming to an end, I can say that school was very fun and a memorable experience to say the least.

When we first started homeschooling, my mom used Connections Academy. Even though this school was online, it wasn't a good fit for me. That's when my mom found out about the Tiers Free Academy homeschool program.

This program differs from any school that I've entered and I was impressed by the structure of the program. For example, I love the fact that students have a whole month to finish one class and on their own time. I also think the program is very well thought out. Let's say a student is having a bad mental health day. They won't be penalized for it as long as they communicate with their course instructors. This allows students to be successful despite setbacks.

The hardest thing about the diploma program, in my opinion, is staying on top of your work because it is very easy to fall off track with the amount of freedom that is provided to us. But being able to work 4 hours a day is your true pathway to success. My advice to other students would be to buy some nice notebooks because writing things down is a better way to help you learn rather than typing up everything. I'd also tell other students to NOT procrastinate. Lastly, do not be afraid to reach out for help. Your instructors are there to answer all questions. I understand being shy but you'd better be safe than sorry.

Sometimes it's hard to believe that I am graduating on May 15, 2021. I am thinking about applying to Atlanta Institute of Music and Media. I would attend for a year and get a feel for the undergraduate school atmosphere and get my Associate's degree. I would then apply to a 4 year university or go discover life. I am very interested in UCLA and Emory School of Medicine. UCLA has the best gymnastics team and I want to put my flexibility and talents to good use. Emory (SOM) on the other hand has perfect opportunities for me to work in the medical field. I am a caring person and very nurturing so I'd like to put that to use for others.

Epilogue

by Dr. Annise Mabry

To say that I am proud of them is an understatement. There are no words to describe what this truly feels like.

Some of my graduates are in the military. Some became police officers, firefighters, or paramedics. Some have graduated from college and are now teachers, counselors, certified peer support specialists, factory workers, airplane mechanics, and diesel mechanics. Some became small business owners. But one title that they will never have again is high school dropout.

When the COVID19 pandemic hit and all of the GED programs had to suspend their in-person classes and testing, my program was the only alternative diploma program in the entire state of Georgia still operating. The reason was: I never designed my program to be face to face—I designed my Tiers Free Academy as an online homeschool program. Back in 2003, when I got my MAEd in Adult and Online Education, I knew that online learning wasn't a fad. It was going to be the new education reality and those who were slow to embrace it would be left behind.

Nothing brought this reality home like the pandemic. I also designed my program for maximum flexibility, accessibility, and portability—three things that struggling adolescents and adult learners need to be successful. Academic trauma is as real as any survivor trauma. Sometimes the simple act of being in a class environment is a trigger for a survivor. I built my program so it would support the student through all and any triggers without handicapping their future success.

It took my lived experience to build a program like this. Lived experience is invaluable. It frustrates me to no end to see people designing something for an entire group of people based on what they think this population needs. Sometimes if you haven't lived it, then leave it alone. Let those with the lived experience build it and then if you are still passionate about supporting that population, support the survivor or the person with the lived experience.

One sad challenge still remains with my academy. My program doesn't receive access to the same level of funding opportunities as a traditional adult literacy program would because nothing about my program is traditional. I built a program for those who never felt like they fit into traditional education or the programs out there. I don't offer classes in a traditional manner nor do I use the traditional metrics of measuring success typically used.

I'm not measuring how many days students come to class. I'm measuring how many students now have an opportunity to change their life as a result of the program. My program success is measured by the number of students who get a high school diploma in 18 months or less and then enroll in technical college, enter the workforce full time in careers earning at least $32,000 per year; or start their own small business.

Some people call me a hero; but, I'm far from a hero. That title is reserved for people face adversity with courage and strength. I took on disrupting the dropout crisis in my community not because I was courageous or strong. I didn't do this because I wanted to but because I had to. It wasn't enough for me to save my children simply because I had the ability to understand homeschool laws and the knowledge of how to build an academic program.

Sometimes when it's quiet at night, I close my eyes and I inhale deeply. As I exhale, I call upon my ancestors to guide my heart. I call upon my daddy to guide my steps. I call upon Helen to guide me to those who need me the most. And I call upon God to protect the hearts and minds of those who need me the most to be open to receive the words that I will speak.

Mary Oliver wrote a poem that asked this question "Tell me, what is it you plan to do with your one wild and precious life?" I'm going to use my one wild and precious life to help homeless LGBTQ youth, sex trafficking survivors, and high school dropouts to get a high school diploma. I'm going to use my one wild and precious life to advocate for the academically invisible and educationally excluded who are often trapped inside of the very boxes that are supposed to protect them.

I'm going to use my one wild and precious life to build a community of box breakers; and, you can too!

The public school system is full of tiers which keep us imprisoned despite our skills and intentions. Join Tiers Free Academy if the public school system has denied your high school diploma through lack of appropriate placement, education plan and anti-bullying policies.

If you are eager to join us or support our journey in anyway, find information on all the ways you can in the next section.

THE TIERS FREE DIFFERENCE

The Tiers Free Difference

Dr. Annise Mabry

One question that I am always asked is "What makes Tiers Free Academy different from other programs?"

For the longest time, I struggled to answer that question. I knew my program was different, but I didn't know how to articulate that difference into words.

When most people decide to start a school, they build it around a specific age group (elementary, middle school, or high school , a gender or an academic focus. None of those things were the driving factor of my program.

I built Tiers Free Academy because my own children were caught in a system of well-intentioned but poorly executed interventions from a century old educational model. I have always said that if you don't know what to do, then put the student in the center of the problem and you will make the right decision. But the reality is few programs are built with the whole student in mind.

When I built the program, I frequently described the program as a pathway to a high school diploma for students who had experienced academic trauma. No one really knew what that meant. But I did. There is some literature now on how to create a trauma-informed classroom. When I started this, however, there was no information on how to build a trauma informed high school academic program.

Our model is focused on empowering the student so that they are not stuck where some academic metric says they should be.

Programs Run by the Tiers Free Academy

ALTERNATIVE DIPLOMA PROGRAM
For lifelong learners, 16+, who aged out (or dropped out) of high school.

CURRICULUM SUPPORT PROGRAM
For parents who want to self-homeschool.
We provide online courses in subject areas.
You maintain records, supervision, & academic oversight.

CHIEF'S DIPLOMA PROGRAM
Housed inside the Oglethorpe Police Department.
Support to any Law Enforcement Agency looking to integrate socialized community policing with facilitating their non-graduate citizen's pathway to a high school diploma.

Other benefits with the Tiers Free Academy

ASSISTING DISABLED STUDENTS

Our program has supported and graduated several students with disabilities.

We facilitate families of special needs students to structure a program around the needs of their student; rather than feeling barricaded by pre-structured, traditional programs.

ASSISTING INCARCERATED OR AT-RISK STUDENTS

The breadth and diversity of content covered by our curriculum options serves both incarcerated and non-incarcerated at-risk student population.

Several schools and school districts are actively using our offered curriculums to serve their
at-risk students in need for a non-traditional experience.

CURRICULUM OPTIONS FOR SMALL/RURAL DISTRICTS

We make our high-level courses and electives to low-budget districts. Availing districts have avoided the extra budget-pressure by optioning our curricular offerings to serve their outlier students.

SUMMER SCHOOL OPTIONS

Our 365 days contracts come with unlimited course availability. School districts have saved budget dollars to open online summer school options to their students via contracting with us.

When students are enrolling in our program, I always ask what are their plans after graduation. Most have no idea what they want to do because they stopped dreaming. That's no surprise coming from a system where tiers, levels, and grades tie up students in knots, telling them their limits, rather than showing them their horizons. That's why we have a grading scale that makes a 60 a "D" and a "D" is passing because sometimes people just need a win.

Our program takes their prior academic transcript and reshapes the narrative from something that felt like a failure to a gateway toward their future. Homeschool programs don't have the restrictions of a public or a private school because there is no accreditation process attached. That means we can free our students from the mentality of the 'shackles'. They stop worrying about where they are at and start focusing on how much they can go forward today. And it's this series of successful todays, ticking their own meter forward one step, one week, and once course at a time, that lets our program achieve carving that path to every student's future..

Since I serve on the accreditation review committees for public and private schools, several accreditation best practices are interwoven into our program design. All of the curriculum that I use in the program has received accreditation but as a program, we do not have accreditation, taking the pressure off the students.

Some people hear this and say "If you aren't accredited then your graduates can't..." Well, if we were a public or a private school, then yes, without accreditation, the graduates' futures would be limited.

As a homeschool program, on the other hand, our graduates can enlist in the military, enroll in college, and qualify for employment just like any other high school graduate.

How we motivate our students is also different. Students work on one class at a time and they are given 30 days to finish that class. I often joke and say "The only thing that I give our students is 30 days to finish a class. They earn the title of high school graduate and every letter on the paper that says High School Diploma."

We Need Your Help!!!

We all hope that their stories will leave you asking, "How can I do more to help?" See, that's why these 14 adults came together to share their stories with you. The COVID19 pandemic wiped out all of our reserve funds to help adults in rural communities obtain their high school diplomas.

The Dr. Annise Mabry Foundation lost 70 monthly donors at the height of the pandemic in March 2020 and those donations haven't returned. In 2021, our largest curriculum vendor implemented a $100 online license minimum at a cost of $10,000 per 100 licenses.

Our diploma program needs funding and the only way that I knew to get this funding was to give the graduates and their parents an opportunity to tell their stories.
All of the proceeds from the sale of this anthology are going into a fund to help the foundation purchase online curriculum licenses.

PayPal is also trying to help to sustain our program and they have created a fundraiser for us. You can donate to the PayPal fundraiser here:
https://www.paypal.com/us/fundraiser/charity/216979

Help us break the box.

Here's How You Can Support Us

Shop using Smile.Amazon.com and select "The Dr. Annise Mabry Foundation"

Become a recurring monthly donor through our Paypal Fundraising Page

Pay the graduation expenses for a graduate

Support us on social media—like our pages and share our posts
Write Nudge Notes (short notes of encouragement that we send the students when we see them struggling online).

Paypal Fundraiser QR Code. Your spare change can literally change a life.

www.ingramcontent.com/pod-product-compliance
Lightning Source LLC
Chambersburg PA
CBHW070800050426
42452CB00012B/2422